This library edition published in 2012 by Walter Foster Publishing, Inc.
Distributed by Black Rabbit Books.
P.O. Box 3263 Mankato, Minnesota 56002

Published by Walter Foster Publishing, Inc.
Walter Foster is a registered trademark.

Printed in Mankato, Minnesota, USA by CG Book Printers, a division of Corporate Graphics.

First Library Edition

Library of Congress Cataloging-in-Publication Data

Martinez, Heather.
  How to draw SpongeBob SquarePants : draw your favorite characters, step by simple step / illustrated by Heather Martinez. -- 1st library ed.
     p. cm. -- (Nickelodeon ; nick11)
  ISBN 978-1-936309-35-1 (hardcover)
  1. Fishes in art--Juvenile literature. 2. Cartoon characters--Juvenile literature. 3. Drawing--Tech-
nique--Juvenile literature. 4. SpongeBob SquarePants (Fictitious character)--Juvenile literature.
  5. SpongeBob SquarePants (Television program)--Juvenile literature. 1. Title. 11. Title: Draw your
favorite characters, step by simple step.
  NC1764.8.F57M37 2011
  741.5'1--dc22
                                                                                      2011008881

022012
17651

9 8 7 6 5 4 3 2

nickelodeon™

How to Draw SpongeBob SquarePants™

Illustrated by
Heather Martinez

Draw your favorite characters, step by simple step

Deep below the ocean, in the undersea city of Bikini Bottom, lives a really well-intentioned yellow sea sponge. His name, like his body, is SpongeBob SquarePants. He always finds himself in hot water without trying too hard... and he's usually not alone. That's because his best friends Patrick Star and Sandy Cheeks are never far behind. Ever the optimist, SpongeBob always makes the best of things (before unintentionally making them worse), and his bubbly attitude and nautical adventures keep Bikini Bottom the most entertaining underwater paradise in the world—and now you can learn how to draw it all!

Walter Foster

Walter Foster Publishing, Inc.
3 Wrigley, Suite A
Irvine, CA 92618
www.walterfoster.com

Line 'em Up!

When cartoonists draw, they pay close attention to a character's *proportions* (the sizes of things compared with things around it). For example, SpongeBob is about twice as tall as Gary but comes up only to Squidward's shoulders. When you're drawing SpongeBob and the other waterlogged residents of Bikini Bottom, you can use this handy height chart to check their proportions.

SpongeBob
Fun-loving SpongeBob is as happy as a clam when he's soaking up bubble art and jelly-fishing in his spare time.

Gary
Gary is SpongeBob's sweet and slimy house pet—a pink-and-blue polka-dotted snail who meows like a cat.

Patrick Star
Even though he's not the smartest star in the sea, Patrick is the most loyal friend and neighbor a sponge could ask for.

Squidward Tentacles
Squidward is easily annoyed by everyone and everything around him, including his nautical neighbor SpongeBob.

Sandy Cheeks
The most (and only) adventurous squirrel in all of Bikini Bottom, Sandy is the ultimate thrill-seeking surfer girl.

Plankton
Plankton is truly tiny compared with the rest of the characters in his watery world, but he is pure, compact evil!

Dive Right In!

SpongeBob and his seaworthy friends are easy to draw—just follow the simple, unsinkable steps! Each new step is shown in blue, so you'll always know what to draw next!

STEP 1

Lightly draw a circle for the top of the bun. Then add two straight lines on the sides and a curved line for the patty and the bottom of the bun.

STEP 2

Add a wavy line for the lettuce and a long oval for the patty.

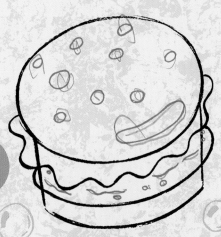

STEP 3

Finish drawing the details—like sesame seeds and grease spots—on the bun and the patty.

STEP 4

Now clean up your pencil lines, erasing any marks you don't need.

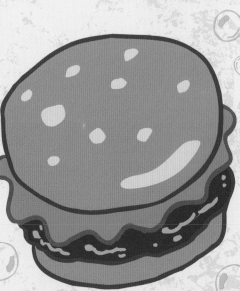

STEP 5

Anchors away! Add some color and your Krabby Patty will look good enough to eat!

4

Fair and Square

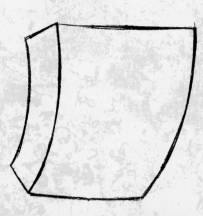

You can tell from his name that SpongeBob SquarePants is as square as they come. Before you dive into drawing our hero and his pals, here are some pointers to get you started off on the right foot.

This is how SpongeBob looks when he's facing you. Notice that the bottom of his square is a little narrower than the top.

With a few additional lines, you can make SpongeBob turn to the side a little. Now he looks more three-dimensional and lifelike.

To make his body bend forward, curve the lines a little more (but leave the top and bottom lines pretty straight).

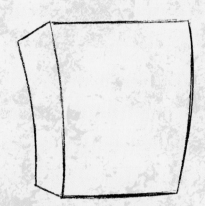

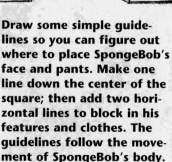

Draw some simple guidelines so you can figure out where to place SpongeBob's face and pants. Make one line down the center of the square; then add two horizontal lines to block in his features and clothes. The guidelines follow the movement of SpongeBob's body.

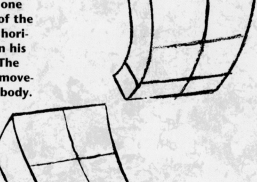

SpongeBob SquarePants

SpongeBob lives in a fully furnished pineapple under the sea with his pet snail Gary. When he's not working hard at The Krusty Krab, he has a lot of interests that keep him occupied: jellyfishing, bubble art, and karate. His never-ending good nature and enthusiasm can often irritate others, but his refreshing attitude makes him a likable underdog. Despite all of his positive traits, "SpongeBob excitement" usually means "SpongeBob disaster." In the end, though, SpongeBob always wins—even if only for himself.

STEP 1

Start with the basic SpongeBob square. Lightly pencil in guidelines for his face and his clothes.

STEP 2

Draw his features. Then add his arms, legs, hands, and feet. Don't forget his shoes, sleeves, and pant legs!

STEP 3

Make the sponge edges wavy. Then finish SpongeBob's eyes and follow the blue lines to add the rest of his spongy details.

SpongeBob's thick eyelashes start at the outer corners of his irises, but they show only above his eyeballs.

SpongeBob's prickly pine-apple palace is a perfectly cozy underwater home.

Make SpongeBob's teeth big and square like this . . .

. . . not long and goofy like this.

STEP 5

Ta-da! Use cray-ons, markers, or colored pencils to finish SpongeBob with bright, bubbly colors—and don't forget his freckled cheeks!

STEP 4

To clean up your drawing, erase any lines you don't need.

When SpongeBob smiles, his cheeks are small and round, with three freckles.

Don't flatten out his cheeks like this.

SpongeBob SquarePants

SpongeBob is the most dedicated employee at the Krusty Krab—he likes his uniform so much that he never takes it off (not even in the shower!). His biggest dream is to capture the prized "Employee of the Month" award—he has won every month.

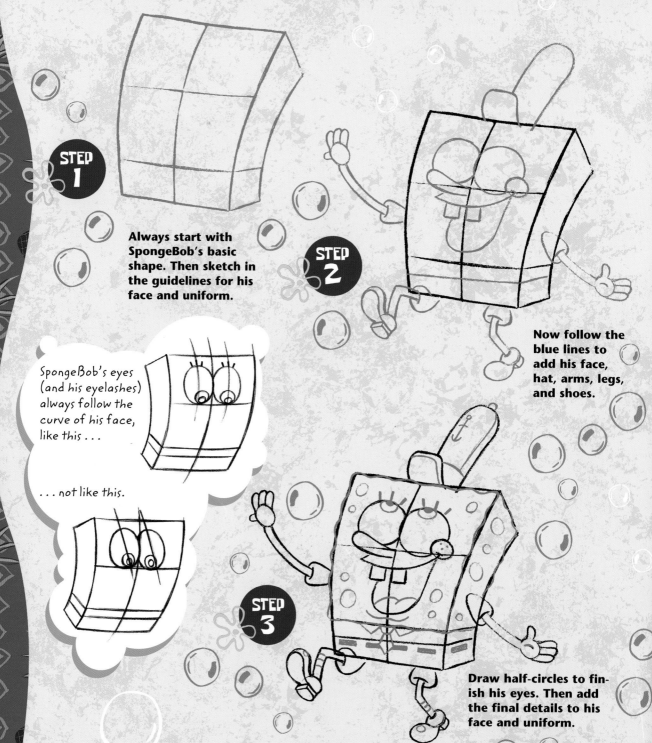

STEP 1

Always start with SpongeBob's basic shape. Then sketch in the guidelines for his face and uniform.

STEP 2

Now follow the blue lines to add his face, hat, arms, legs, and shoes.

SpongeBob's eyes (and his eyelashes) always follow the curve of his face, like this . . .

. . . not like this.

STEP 3

Draw half-circles to finish his eyes. Then add the final details to his face and uniform.

SpongeBob never has more than two top teeth.

Perfect!

Not like this . . .

. . . or like this.

STEP
5

Now color your drawing. Then try adding some waterlogged stuff for SpongeBob to juggle!

STEP
4

Now clean up your pencil lines and erase the guidelines.

SpongeBob's Shoes

Draw a small ball around the base of his leg.

Then make a simple shape for the front of the shoe.

Add the heel; don't forget the highlight on the toe!

This is what his shoe looks like from the bottom.

Patrick Star

Patrick is SpongeBob's dim-witted yet loyal best friend. His hobbies include sleeping and lying still. This starfish truly idolizes SpongeBob, and together they make a mess of things for everyone around them—but always without meaning to. Part sloth and part dude, Patrick's biggest ambition in life is "uh . . . I . . . uh . . . forget."

When Patrick uses his hands, they look like mittens. Be sure to keep them very simple.

holding something

making a fist

pointing

waving good-bye

STEP 1

STEP 2

Start with a big teardrop shape for Patrick's body. Then add the guidelines for his face and his shorts.

Patrick's eyebrows look like two thick "Z's" squished together . . .

. . . like this . . .

. . . not like this. Don't make them too thin!

Draw rounded triangle shapes for his arms and legs. Then add his eyes and mouth.

Patrick's flowery pants look the same from the front and back. There's one large flower in the middle and one smaller flower on each side.

Now erase any pencil lines you don't need.

Follow the blue lines to add his trunks and the rest of the details on his face and body. Don't forget his belly button!

When Patrick is really angry or scared, he shows his round teeth!

Color Patrick's tropical trunks seaweed green. Then outline his body in red.

Gary

SpongeBob often confides in his favorite companion and pet—Gary, the snail. Gary may meow like a cat, but the slimy trail he leaves behind definitely proves he's a mollusk.

When you draw all the characters' eyelids (especially Gary's) make them thick like this.

Don't flatten them out like this!

STEP 1

Draw an egg shape for Gary's shell and an oval with a flat bottom for his body.

STEP 2

Now add his two antennae, his mouth, and the wavy line under his belly.

STEP 3

Make circles for his eyes. Then add his lips and all the details on his shell and body.

When Gary is scared, he tucks in his antennae like this.

STEP 4

Finish up by erasing your guidelines and cleaning up your pencil lines.

STEP 5

If you want an even outline, trace over your pencil lines with a fine-tipped black marker. Then add some magnificent color to meowing Gary!

SpongeBob in Action

Every SpongeBob pose follows one basic line that defines the action. Use the action tips below to create super, action–soaked drawings!

The curve that starts at the top of the character's head and goes to the feet is called the "line of action" (or "action line").

In these poses, the position of SpongeBob's arms and legs creates secondary lines of action.

Even when he's just standing around, SpongeBob has a slightly curved line of action.

Keep the curve when you draw SpongeBob's face. It's very expressive and "animated"—a face in action!

Here Gary's line of action creates the perfect balance to SpongeBob's pose.

Squidward Tentacles

Co-worker and neighbor of SpongeBob, Squidward is a bitter and obnoxious octopus. Everyone and everything annoy him—except his own clarinet playing and painting. This could be because Squidward is two arms short of a full set of tentacles.

Squidward's rectangular pupils follow the curve of his eye like this . . .

. . . not flat like this.

His lips are thick and droopy at the edges.

STEP 2

STEP 1

Start with basic shapes to create Squidward's head and body.

When Squidward walks, his four legs pair off and move together.

Now draw his eyes, nose, and arms—and the two extra tentacles for his legs.

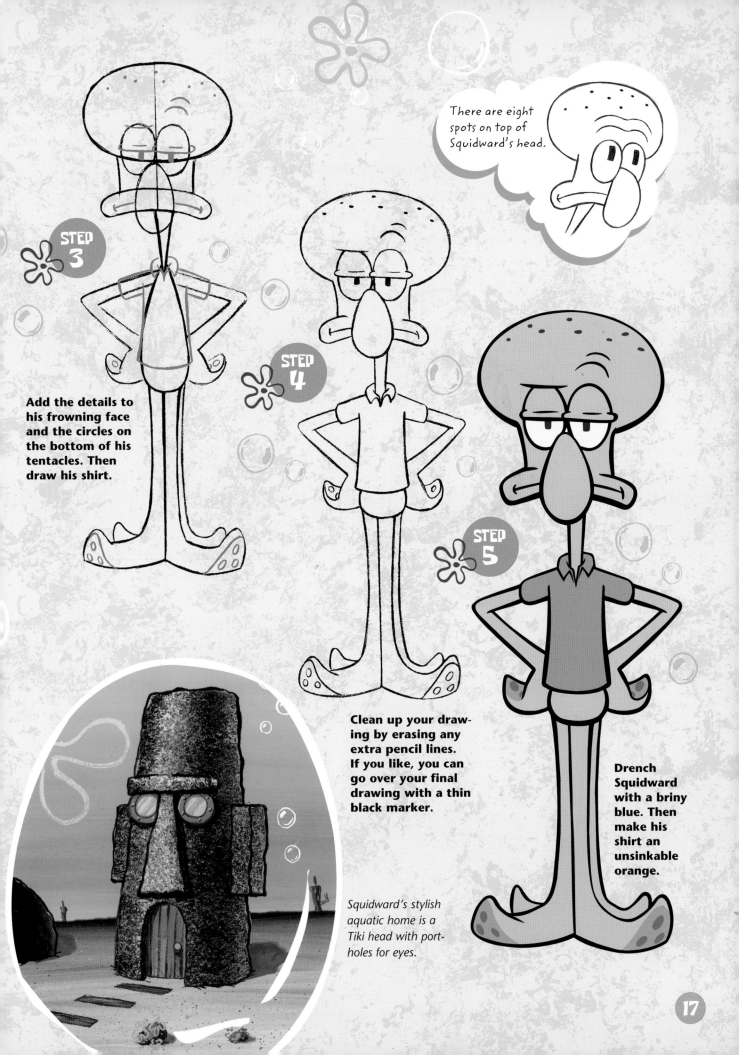

There are eight spots on top of Squidward's head.

Add the details to his frowning face and the circles on the bottom of his tentacles. Then draw his shirt.

STEP 4

STEP 5

Clean up your drawing by erasing any extra pencil lines. If you like, you can go over your final drawing with a thin black marker.

Drench Squidward with a briny blue. Then make his shirt an unsinkable orange.

Squidward's stylish aquatic home is a Tiki head with port-holes for eyes.

17

Sandy Cheeks

Active and athletic, this Texas-born squirrel is taking the ultimate challenge by living underwater. When she's not lifting weights or practicing karate, Sandy often brings SpongeBob along on one of her thrill-seeking adventures.

STEP 2

Then add her arms and legs, face and neck, and finally her air helmet.

STEP 1

Begin with a cylinder shape for Sandy's body. Then draw a simple bean shape and a rounded square for her head.

Sandy's teeth are square. The line in the middle goes only halfway down from the top like this . . .

. . . not like this. Be sure you don't make her teeth too long.

When Sandy is in her air dome, she sports a bikini.

The only time Sandy can take off her helmet is when she's at home in her air dome.

Sandy's tail sticks out of the back of her suit. Start with the basic shape. Then add three tufts of fur.

STEP 3

Next follow the blue lines to add all the details that make Sandy so spunky—and don't forget her flower!

STEP 4

Erase any extra pencil lines and guidelines.

STEP 5

Now color Sandy's suit white and her body brown. Then outline her helmet in white to show how transparent it is.

Here are some other views of Sandy's boots.

19

Mr. Krabs

Mr. Krabs is the greedy owner of the Krusty Krab and SpongeBob's money-hungry boss. Though he finds SpongeBob a constant source of aggravation, Mr. Krabs genuinely likes him. The only thing more valuable to Mr. Krabs than cold, hard cash is his teenage daughter Pearl.

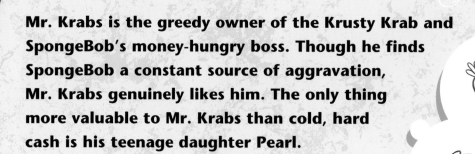

Notice that Mr. Krabs' long, tear-shaped eyes can be very expressive.

Use short lines to separate his square teeth.

STEP 1

Start with a triangle with rounded edges.

STEP 2

Then follow the blue lines to add his antennae, claws, and feet. Now draw the curved guidelines for his pants and belt.

The Krusty Krab—home of the Krabby Patty, salty shakes, and coral fries—is the most popular fast-food joint in Bikini Bottom.

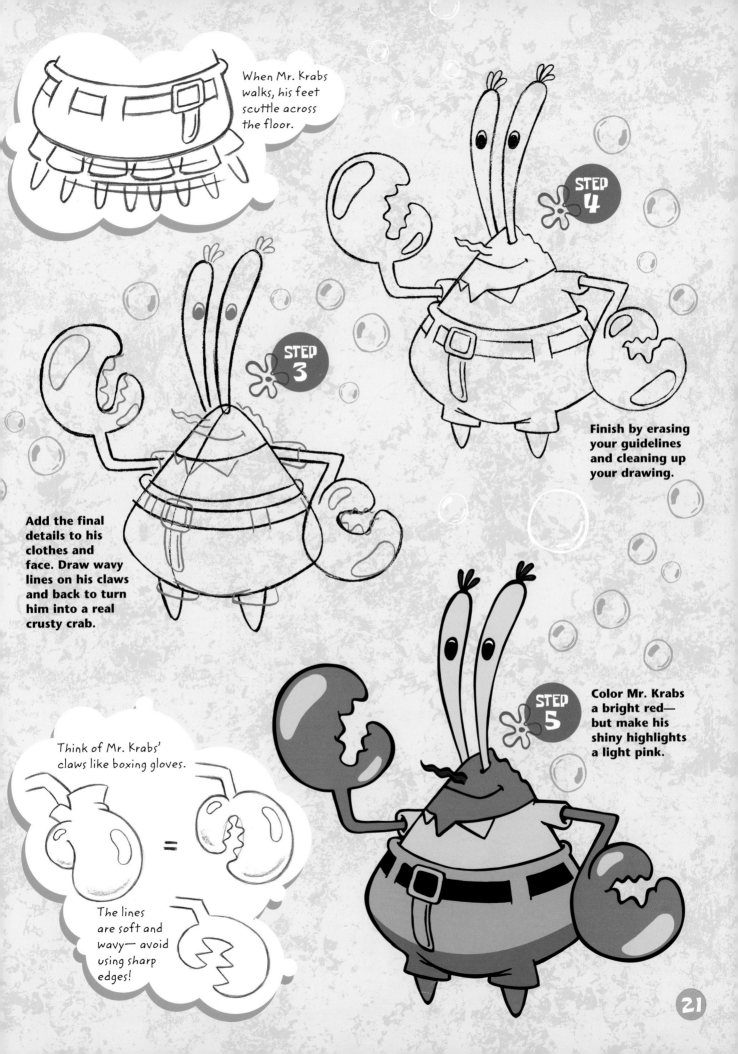

When Mr. Krabs walks, his feet scuttle across the floor.

Finish by erasing your guidelines and cleaning up your drawing.

Add the final details to his clothes and face. Draw wavy lines on his claws and back to turn him into a real crusty crab.

Color Mr. Krabs a bright red—but make his shiny highlights a light pink.

Think of Mr. Krabs' claws like boxing gloves.

The lines are soft and wavy— avoid using sharp edges!

Pearl

Like most other teenage girls, Pearl loves shopping, music, and boys. But Pearl also has the biggest brain in Bikini Bottom, and she's great at math—too bad she throws a lot of salty-teared tantrums when she doesn't get what she wants.

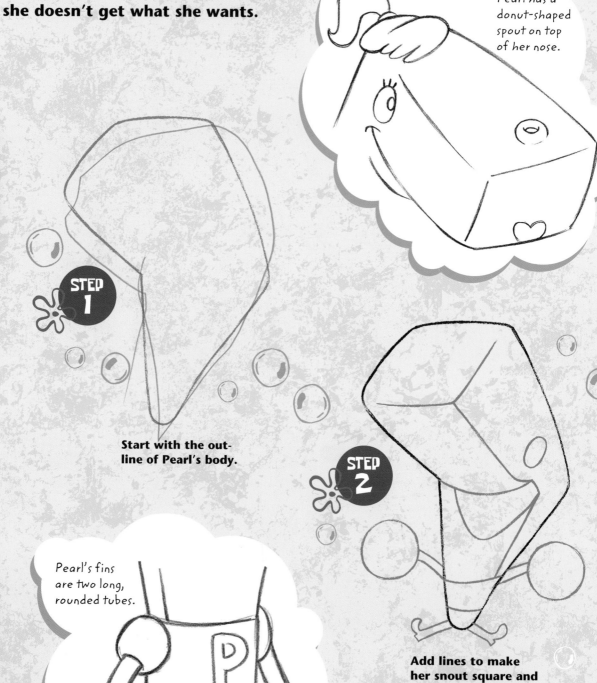

Pearl has a donut-shaped spout on top of her nose.

STEP 1

Start with the outline of Pearl's body.

STEP 2

Add lines to make her snout square and circles for her pompoms. Then draw the details of her face and body.

Pearl's fins are two long, rounded tubes.

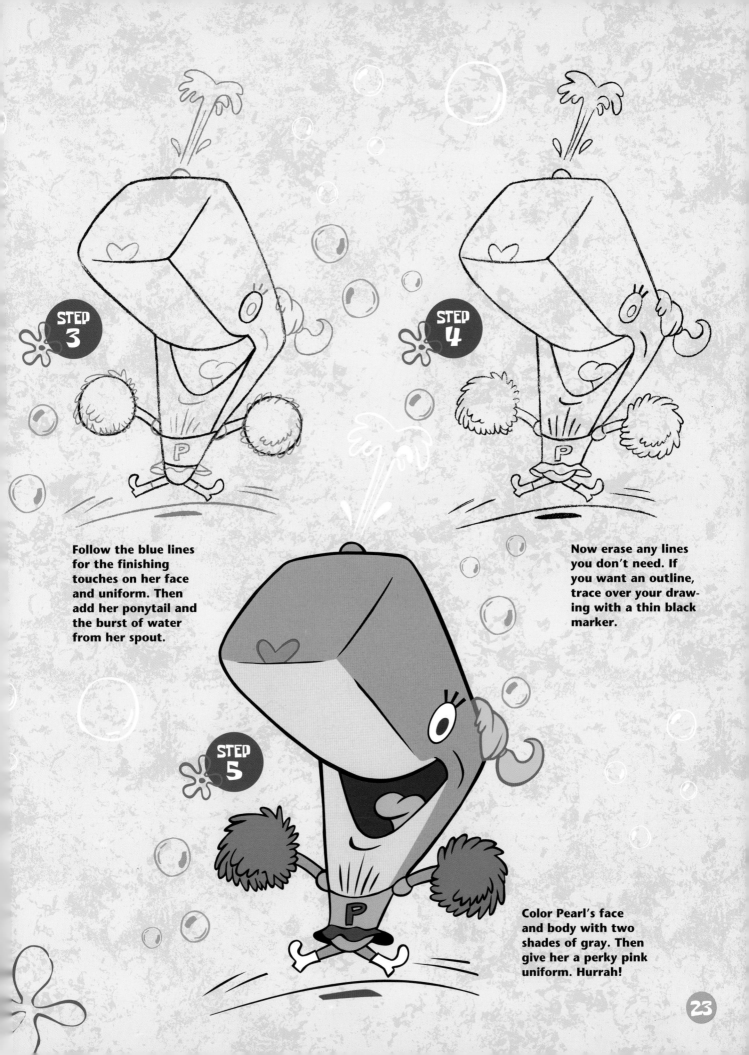

STEP 3

Follow the blue lines for the finishing touches on her face and uniform. Then add her ponytail and the burst of water from her spout.

STEP 4

Now erase any lines you don't need. If you want an outline, trace over your drawing with a thin black marker.

STEP 5

Color Pearl's face and body with two shades of gray. Then give her a perky pink uniform. Hurrah!

Plankton

Plankton owns Plankton's Chum Bucket, the Krusty Krab's rival. And business isn't good. Boastful and mean, Plankton is constantly plotting ways to steal the famous Krabby Patty recipe.

STEP 1

Start with a slightly curved oval for Plankton's briny body.

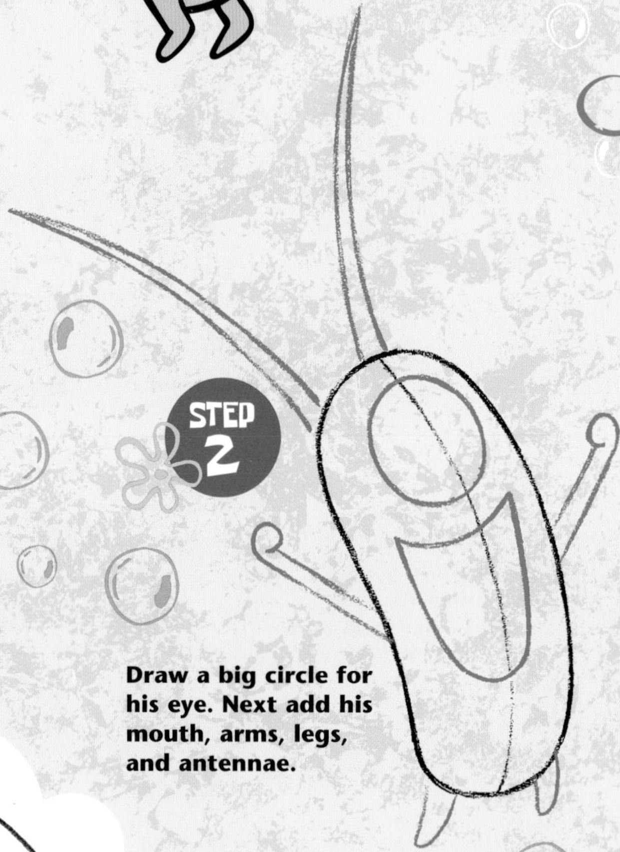

STEP 2

Draw a big circle for his eye. Next add his mouth, arms, legs, and antennae.

When you draw Plankton, don't forget that he's very, very small!

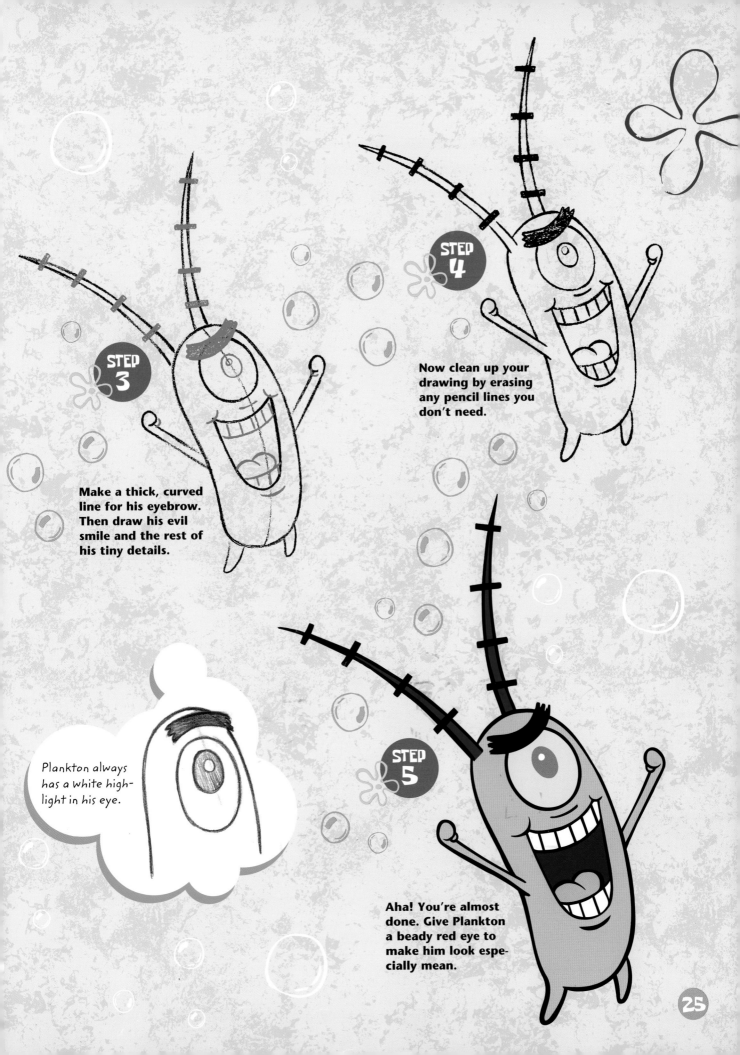

STEP 3

Make a thick, curved line for his eyebrow. Then draw his evil smile and the rest of his tiny details.

STEP 4

Now clean up your drawing by erasing any pencil lines you don't need.

Plankton always has a white high-light in his eye.

STEP 5

Aha! You're almost done. Give Plankton a beady red eye to make him look especially mean.

Mrs. Puff

Mrs. Puff would like nothing more than to have SpongeBob pass his boat-driving exam (he's taken the test at least 47 times). This Bikini Bottom Boating School teacher is a puffer fish; when she gets excited, her body expands to many times its normal size. Watch out!

STEP 2

Draw two curved guidelines for her dress. Then add her fins, feet, face, and hair.

STEP 1

To draw Mrs. Puff, begin with a large, egg-shaped oval.

Here's Mrs. Puff when she's all puffed up.

Mrs. Puff's teeth are similar to Squidward's— soft lines and round edges.

Finish by erasing your guidelines and any stray pencil marks.

Follow the blue lines to draw her hat and ruler. Then add the details on her face, fins, dress, and body.

Color Mrs. Puff's dress and hat with bubbly blue and splashy scarlet red.

Jellyfish

These calm, spineless wonders spend their days floating without a care through Jellyfish Fields. But when SpongeBob and Patrick go jellyfishing, the fish change into savage, stinging beasts who can be tamed only by music.

Jellyfish have a powerful, electric sting.

STEP 1

Start with an oval and a curve for the basic body of the jellyfish.

STEP 2

Draw four long, thin, wavy tubes for tentacles.

Jellyfishing (which is like catching butterflies) is a popular sport in Bikini Bottom.

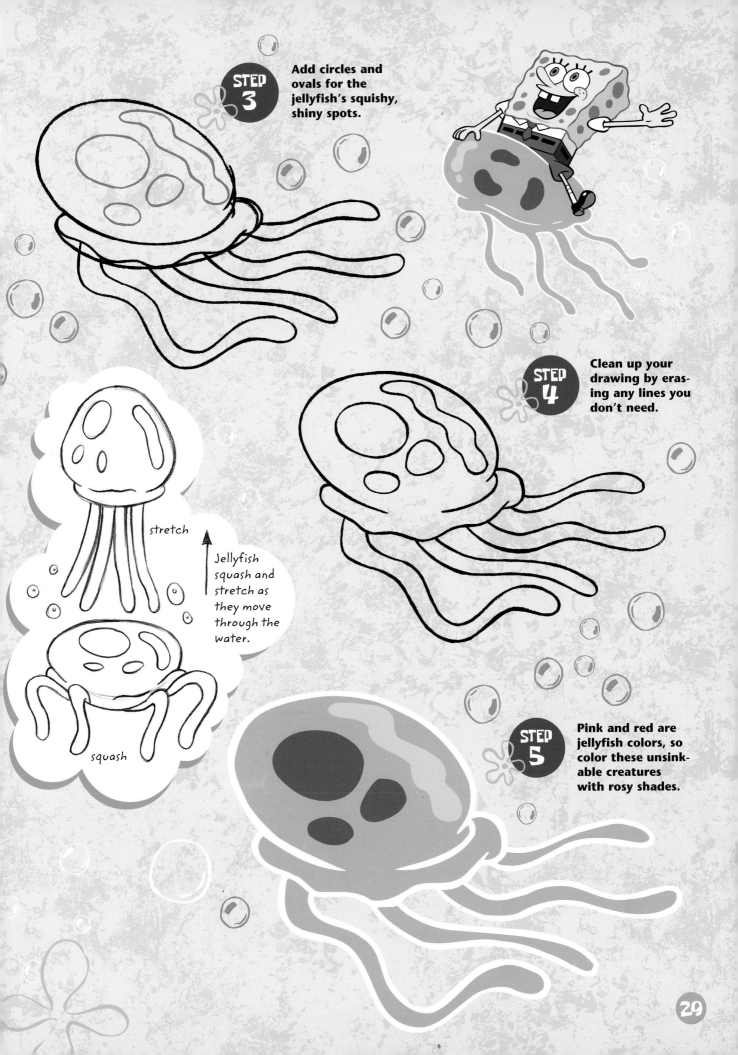

STEP 3

Add circles and ovals for the jellyfish's squishy, shiny spots.

STEP 4

Clean up your drawing by erasing any lines you don't need.

stretch

Jellyfish squash and stretch as they move through the water.

squash

STEP 5

Pink and red are jellyfish colors, so color these unsinkable creatures with rosy shades.

Seaworthy Stories

Ahoy, matey! Now you can put all the nautical knowledge you've soaked up into action by writing and illustrating your own absorbent SpongeBob adventures. Use your bubbly imagination to dream up what SpongeBob and his pals will do next. Get creative, get silly, and get started!

Make me the hero of your story!

STEP 1

Before you begin, plan out your story. Then sketch out what will happen on each action-packed page.

Front Cover

"Would you play Hide-and-Seek with us, Squidward?" asks SpongeBob.

Squidward gets an idea. "OK, I'll play! You guys go hide," he says.

Page 1   Page 2

"Playing with Squidward will be fun!" laughs SpongeBob.

"Those fools will be hiding for hours while I'm inside resting," says Squidward.

Page 3   Page 4

"Time for my Beauty Nap," says Squidward.

"You found us! Now it's your turn to hide!"

Page 5   Page 6

Back Cover

To make your book, fold a large, blank piece of paper in half. Then fold it in half again.

Staple along the second fold to create the book's spine.

Trim off the edges of the remaining two folds.

Now write, draw, and color in your nautical tale.

Share your splashy story with friends—and soak up their admiration.

Sail Away

Don't stop here! Keep drawing our sailorific hero and his salty pals into many more nautical adventures. Go overboard—and have fun!